Brittiny Gardner

From Me to You

Wider Perspectives Publishing ∞ 2023 ∞ Norfolk, Va.

© 2023, Brittiny Gardner,
1st run complete in September 2023
Wider Perspectives Publishing, Hampton Roads, Va.
ISBN 978-1-952773-79-2

Dedicated

None of you would be reading this book today
if it wasn't for
all you've said and done in my life.
All of you have imprinted upon me.

So from me to you:

Thank You

Forgiven Over Time

If I look into your eyes
Will you see the pain of my past
Will you understand?

When you see me cry
Will you ever see why
I was willing to change
To do more than just rearrange
To put on yet another skin
To be loved, valued, and accepted in

When you saw me smile
Saw my light for the first time
You burned it out
You covered my mouth
Silenced my voice
And told me that I had no choice

If I smile at you now
You'll see my light for the first time
In a long time
Will you realize what you did to me then?

When you saw me laugh
I would feel the slap before it came
I would feel the daggers before they hit
I would see my fantasy ripped apart in front of me
A dismal reminder of my reality

When you see me now
You treat me as if I am a stranger
No longer afflicted from your anger
No longer afraid to use my voice
No longer worried if I have a choice

If you understood what you did to me then
You'd be surprised at the response
I give to you now

Thank you

Thank you for the pain and the poison
Thank you for the lies and the secrets
Thank you for brainwashing me and
Keeping me inside my box
Thank you for my past

What you did to me
What you said to me
What you allowed to happen
What you chose to forget
Helped me fight for my life

I'm a fighter
I'm stubborn
I'm compassionate
I'm caring
I'm a writer that writes with her whole heart

I may be damaged
I may have bad self esteem
I may have a hard time with the real world
I may be skittish and afraid through people's eyes.

But I am in a better place
I'm growing at my own pace
I'm shedding skin
And coming into my own
I no longer feel lost and alone

When you see me cry
When you see me smile
When you hear me laugh
I want you to know
You played your role in all of that

If I look into your eyes
If I smile at you now
If I could show you the road
I traveled since I left
I'd tell you this
'I took the road less traveled by, and that has made all the difference,'

Brittiny Gardner

The Booth

It was five years ago
On the phone
You told me it had hit you
Square in the chest
You told me it had happened recently
While you were inside of Denny's

You said
Giving up a habit
Is like no longer following the rabbit
Down its rabbit hole
Towards Wonderland
Full of creative imagery
Full of possibility
A perfect medicated symmetry
Are you following me?

(I nodded yes from across the ocean)

You said
Giving up a habit
Is like losing something when
You never really had it
A craving
A solace
An escape
Wondering how much of it you can take

(All I could think was—where are you going with this?)

From Me

You continued
Giving up a habit
Breathe
Giving up a habit
Taking the first step
Giving up a habit
Wishing I had been to my then 12-year-old daughter's singing recital
Giving up a habit
Wishing I had gone to watch my then 10-year-old son beat his school's
rival
Giving up a habit
Upset I had lost my temper on your mom
And you kids repeatedly
Exhale
Giving up a habit
Accepting I have an addiction

(My heart was aching on the other end.
 His words
Our past
The thread tightening our bond again
I held the welling tears at bay
I needed to hear what else he had left to say)

He said
Giving up an addiction
That's when it hit me
Sitting in a booth at Denny's
When I witnessed a father daughter date
A little girl around seven pushing pancakes around on her plate

The two of them
Smiling
Laughing
Talking
I could feel my sudden anger
I could feel the tears
And when they fell
I saw my reflection in the mirror

He said
I saw the better version
Of what I wanted to be
I saw the father
You'd always known I could be
He took a breath
"Bird, I'm sorry I'm 20 years late,
But could we, possibly, one day
Have a father daughter date?"

With my own tears now free flowing
From the other end
My mouth dry
My tongue tied
Part of me demanding inside my head
"Why. Why now, not then?"
I found myself saying out loud
"Dad, when I can take leave we'll make it happen,"

The Past, Present, and Future Me

May the first
I crossed the threshold
After sharing my poem
I finally after 25 years
Have started to Let Go

So why then do I still have that same dream?
The one where I'm in a dark room
And there's a spotlight on me?

The one where a frightened little girl
She looks right at me
And then back behind her
Clutching her book tightly to her chest
As if that would protect her

People say as you age
Your eyes are the only parts of you
That don't change
And as I stare at this fragile girl
Her wild hazel eyes boring into my own

I've never felt so broken, so angry before
The bruises on her neck
And the scars all over her body
Mirrored my own permanent ones
I nearly came undone

At one point she tentatively moves
Then pulls back
Looks back
Crying
She looks at me
Mouthing, "Help Me,"
She reaches for me

And then we both hear the sound
The sound that caused those scars
The sound that created her bruises
The sound that had us both breathing fast
Knowing what was coming next

I broke from my own fear
Rushing over to her
Gathering her into my arms
Holding onto her tightly
Shushing her cries

Telling her she's much stronger than she thinks
That these bruises and scars
They'll wind up carrying us far
They'll help us blossom into who we are
That they don't make us look weak
That they don't make us used
Damaged
Abused
They help us know we survived
That we made it through.

As she trembles in my arms
Her crying turns to rage
Her little fists
Hitting me in the chest
I knew why
She knew why
But I held onto her for as long as I could until then

Until the sound came
And tore her away from me
And I was left hearing her screaming cries
Bleeding my ears from the inside
Causing me to drop
Cry my own unspent tears
As I felt ripped apart
Only to wake up
May the first
I crossed the threshold
After sharing my poem
Finally after 25 years
I have started to let go

But the little girl inside of me
She can never forget
She can't truly forgive
She's hurt and angry
She's worried and scared
Where I wish I could tell her
We made it
We're ok

She's still enduring the darkness
And the past bitter pain
I know
For myself
Letting go is the start
But I can't do this alone
So if you've been touched by this poem
Know that this is the most I have ever
Been vulnerable
Been raw
Been real
And I hope you take this
And empower and reassure that
Little girl or boy still inside of you
Hold onto them tightly
Love them
Be with them
Be there for them when they needed someone desperately
Help them to see
There is comfort through suffering.

Once Upon A Time

Instead of my 4-year-old hands
Continuing rapping on the door
Until they bled
Hearing the screams coming from the other side of the door
My sister
Like an angel
Whisked me away that night
Introducing me
To a much happier time
A moment to escape
To watch an actual happy ending take place
That was the night I discovered Disney
When I laughed and sang along to
"Under the Sea,"

At 6 or 7,
I learned the horror of the
Evil frightening
Blue monkeys from the Wizard of Oz
But I also learned about Pizza Planet,
"To infinity and Beyond!"
Singing along to
"You've Got a Friend in Me,"
All while potentially hiding from
The future fire
The future lie
That would haunt me for years
The spillage of blood and tears

While my young innocence danced and sang
Every Disney song
I wanted to believe in a happily ever after
That could be everlasting long.

When I was 12,
I sang, "A Spoonful of Sugar,"
And I won the contest
But I never saw my parents
Cheering me on
Smiling or clapping
No
They were back home
Bitter or napping

At 13,
I got the Disney Princess itis
Where I wanted a prince
With a perfect jawline
To come and rescue me
When I wanted to run away
Like Belle and Jasmine
A yearning to be free
To discover "A Whole New World,"
Somewhere fun and fancy free

When I was 16,
Taking mythology
Learning about heroes journeys
We rewatched the Lion King
And it hit me then

When Rafiki bopped Simba on the head
"The past can hurt. But the way I see it,
        you can either run from it or learn from it,"
Such a revelation after that
Disney once again was
Preparing me
Saving me
Helping me
Find me.

After 17,
When the dark completely swallowed me
When the pain grew unbearable
When the puppet wanted to cut her strings
She did
She severed those marionette wires
She cried out for a better life
Just like Disney channel
A Cinderella Story
High School Musical
She just wanted to believe in something beautiful.

At 20,
I signed my name
Took the path of Belle, Jasmine, of Rapunzel and Jane
I ran away
I look back from time to time
I forgave but never forgot
This poem is meant to alleviate
But also to appreciate
Disney

to You

For my childhood innocence
It got me through to here today
My own Mulan history
My own storytelling way
I am grateful my sister
Showed me a happier ending
That long ago night
For without Disney being a huge part of my life
I truly wonder if I would've turned out all right.

The Rush

Breathe
Get a grip
Biting my lip
Is it bleeding again?
Man, damn, there I go again
That heat
That beat
That smile
Those eyes
My mind
No way, let go
Heart racing now
Does he feel the same?
Does he have a hard time grappling our reality
He's so close
Yet so far
Breathe
Drum cacophony going on in my heart right now
Inches
Centimeters
Nose to nose
Mouths teasingly close
Breathe
Compressed
Wild sparks
Drug like feelings
Addicting
Caution to the wind
I regret nothing.

Modern Myth

Cupid is Aphrodite's son
He fell in love with Psyche
Tested, she won his love
He won her
Her heart
Her soul
Her body
Her own "Psyche,"
Sex in itself deals with the three
Cupid with his love torn passion
Psyche with her connection and emotion
Aphrodite using love with all her endearing and horrifying qualities
Desire
Craving
Intuition
Lust
The lotus flower that man can eat and not be trapped
Forever in time
In déjà vu
In love lust passion
To frail eternity once awaken
Sex is to be
Loved
Understood
Fun and free giving
A lasting Greek tale like
Cupid and Psyche
A lasting arrow
Shot from Cupid's own bow

A lasting truth
To believe in
To hope for one day
To have forever after.

Love Inked

You're the man
I'll write songs about
Torrid love
Passionate forbearance
Lasting tears
Hearts crushed to dust
Souls in agony

You're the man
In my books
In my dreams
Hair black as midnight
Eyes cast full of intellect
Skin pale and soft
Laughter
Memories
History
Forever imprinted in future ink

You're the man
Who stole my heart
Who stole my kisses
Who stole my sanity
Who stole my pain
Who began healing me
Who I loved forever and a day

And will forever more
You're the Beast to my Belle

The Rhett to my Scarlett
It just took me time
Too late
Heartache
A permanent ink date.

Gray Dawn

Complete exhaustion
Complete pride
Hope in the dark
Still cracking the flint
Hoping for some fire
Hoping for some light
Gray skies
Kissing rain
Inspiration.

Beautiful Thread

Truth
Inspires
Creativity
Enlightens
Innovation
Progresses
Humanity
Beautiful
Soul
Mind
Cogs
Heart
Strings
Time
Distance
Love
Abides
Inspiration

Inner Strength

I regret nothing
I can say I have lived
I can say I have loved
My wrinkles show how often
I smiled
I laughed
My eyes
Show you the spark
The grief
The determination
The pain
The strength
The peace of mind I have always yearned for
Throughout all of my life
I have been hurt
But I forgave
I have quit on myself in frustration
But I always bounced back
As long as you try
You'll end up like me
Living with no regrets.

Boys

Boys
treat girls like used and unused toys
Boys
are immature
they only see the big picture
they don't notice the little details
which leads them down a bad trail
Boys
always think they're on top
but us women want them to stop
stop trying to beat everyone
stop trying to impress
only for us women to receive less and less
to be tricked
by some superficial dick
Boys
need to go
Men
need to show those boys
how to grow up
shut up
step up
jump up and smile
live, laugh, and love every once in awhile
be true to you
and you'll be closer to becoming a man
continue being anything else, anyone else
you may as well title yourself
Boy

to You

Same Idea

Boys aim to conquer
Girls aim to please
Men conquer
Women please
Through the centuries
There may be a lot of change
But this idea remains the same
Boys aim to conquer
Men conquer
Girls aim to please
Women please—men's ideology.

Déjà vu

Death
Déjà vu
Destiny
Fate
Eternal weaving
Born again threads
Over and over and over again
Past
Present
Future
Faith
Science
Interior realities
Minor factors
Change

Webbing
Threading
Forming
Breaking
Life
Time
Constant
Spent
Wasted
Earned
Death
Déjà vu
Destiny
Fate
A plan
And it cycles over again

Fated Love

Love is
An ocean deep
A passionate flame
A box of chocolates
A small seed
An invisible thread
Good
Evil
Unsure
Too sure
Half of one
Half of the other
Fate
Destiny
A dream
A reality
Forever an unsolved mystery
Is love.

Rooted Love

Despite all the odds
Despite all the pain to follow
Despite all the disappointed and angry looks
Despite all of the tears
Despite all of the packing and moving
Despite all of the years coming and going
Despite the growth of you both
Despite the growth of your children
Despite all of the pointless arguments
Despite all of the persisting doubt
You both stay rooted
You both grow and branch off
You thrive for as long
As you both can survive
That's Love's Enduring Promise.

Heartache

Letting go
It's all you do
Running away
It's all you know
The aftermath
The never ending hurt
It's all you go through
Everlasting heartache.

Home Sweet Home

Different roasts
Different coasts
Same cups
Same atmosphere
Same friendly smiles
A second home
The coffee shop
Better than a bar hop
Comfier than a night clubbing
The sweet morning aroma
Tickling your nose
You're home
Home sweet home
Once that cup is in your hands
You're free to travel different lands
Escape
Be free
Drink your deserved coffee.

Song of the Sea

Music is like the sea
The current is always changing
Much like the notes of a song
The waves mist the hair in your face
Like the music tingles the hairs on your arms
The seas can be calm and soothing
Like listening to a lullaby or a tune of serenity
Music and the sea
They have a beautiful dangerous harmony.

Reliving History

Revolution
Execution
Declaration
Revelation
Ambition
Condition
Contrition
Rendition
I'm calling for auditions!
Same song
Same dance
History repeats itself
Chance after chance
The hands of fate
Times and dates
The only things that ever change
The beginning
The middle
The end
Shall I tell it all over again?
Revolution
Execution
Declaration
Revelation

Ambition
Condition
Contrition
Rendition
Monarchy
Anarchy
Diplomacy
The roles we play
Give or sway
Create change
Surrender over to tradition
History repeats itself
Chance after chance
The hands of fate
Times and dates
The only things that ever change
Blood sheds
Death grows
See all the heads roll!
Liberty
Equality
Society
Reality

Different lists
Different instruments of death
Different people
Different ideals
Same fears
Same roles
Same song
Same dance
History repeats itself
Chance after chance
An eternal rooted stance
Retribution
Persecution
Reason
Treason
Fires
Pyres
Liars
Criers
Black lists
Clenched fists
Secrets
Lyrics

Songs we sing
Dances we bring
Love
Loss
All at a great cost
All lost
History
Found
Bound
Sound
Crowned
Repeating itself
Chance after chance
Same song
Same dance
Look around…

The First Cut is the Deepest

An ache I can't name
A heart that will never be the same
Sleepless
Restless
Hopeless
Reckless
I still have his necklace
I gave the sea my engagement ring
I still have the memories
Now a tattooed reality
The ink is felt every day
Like a new inking
All these feelings
Depression
Sadness
Anger
Confusion
Leave me in a wishful delusion
And the only remedy
The only conclusion
To let it hurt
To give it time
Watch my body get sick
Listen to my heart break
Hear the constant support
The advice
To move on with my life
To cry a little
To let it go

To get over it
I fear I'll never get over it
You entered my life when I was lost
The both of us damaged
The both of us entombed in our own pain
Then the rainbow showed after the rain
There was a first aid kit for our hearts
We gave pieces to each other
Sewed them in
Never thinking they'd become a painful bandage
A reminder of
What could've been
What should've been
What might've been
If we'd only opened up more to each other
If you'd listened more
If I'd been honest with my feelings
If you had told me the truth
Our trust faltered
Then split
The fire that was once lit
Became nothing but a pit of ash
And for a long time
On and off
We tried relighting that match
Catching the spark from long ago
Only to burn ourselves in the process
Burn us
Heal us
Leave us hopeless
And instead of fighting as I did for you

At your worst
You chose to walk away
Leave me crying in the dirt
An ache I can't name
A heart that will never be the same
Sleepless
Restless
Hopeless
The spark extinguished.

Reflection

You never understood me
Even though you tried
All my feelings I harbored very deep inside
And when they'd chance to surface
You didn't know what to do
All you wanted was for me to be like you

We had our highs and lows
Love in us continued to grow
Eventually it grew to be too much
So our love now lies in a dirty dusty rut

I still care for you a great deal
But you've left me to begin to heal
For yourself
For myself
We chose distance
We chose no words
No verbal exchanges
We want our own changes
I never understood you
Even though I tried
All the pain of your past of who you are
You buried deep inside
And when you opened up to me
I was full of empathy
All I wanted was to set you free
From your poisoned misery

Now as I think on my own
I know it's better being alone
It's teaching me
Healing me
Helping me
Break the cycle
Change my fate
Open my eyes
But wall up my heart
It's been brutalized

I'm beginning to heal
I'm beginning to see
I never understood you
You never understood me
We pretended
We changed for the other
Only for our flame to be smothered
Snuffed out
Ashes in the wind
Of what should've
What could've
What might've beens

Today I release you from my heart
Today I breathe in and out
Today I feel like myself
Today I want nothing more of the past
Today I finally feel free at last.

One Step at a Time

She shouts at the distance in front of her
She falls down to her bare knees
She's covered in scratches
Each cut too deep
Each scar a memory
Each a mark of her journey
Her tears fall to the ground before her
Her eyes madly searching in vain
Where was she to go now
From whence she just came
What path should she now take
No voices in her ears
No premonition dreams
No feelings or inklings
Everything barren and unseen
The unknown held her back
The uncertainty breaks her heart
The fear of what she was to do
Where to go
How to get there
Lost her once knowing smile
Lost her grip on reality
Lost her identity
The past
She looks back
The present
She looks down
The future
She looks ahead

Where will her journey take her now
Will she ever learn to accept her scars
Accept her imperfections
Accept her past which led her to the present
Will she ever learn to simply
Breathe
Believe
And one day soon receive?
Will she ever understand that it's ok
To be imperfect
To ask questions
To be curious
To want to learn
Will she ever love herself
And be whole again
Herself again
Free again
Whatever this next leg of her journey
She will find peace of mind
She will set her own self free
She will reclaim her identity
As long as God is guiding her, and she is listening.

Forever and a Day

Always I'll regret when
I never said all I wanted to say
I couldn't hold on after that nightmarish day
I said I'd love him
For forever and a day
To this day
I've kept my word
To this day
He's never heard
Just how much I went through
To this day
He'll never know
How many tears I shed
And continue to
How often I smile or get mad
Whenever I think about him.

Stay

Therein lies a broken heart
It has been patched
And stitched
And bandaged
It has been torn
And burned
And beaten
So there it lays, mourning
Each and every day
For the people it loved
Who walked away
When within a single heart beat
The girl whose heart lay broken
She
She would've stayed.

Fragile

Please don't use me
As your remedy
As your muse
As your plastic utensil to toss away

Please don't manipulate me
Through playing with my emotions
Through pretending to care
Through your own means to an end

Please don't hurt me
Not today
Not anymore
Never again

Please don't lie to me
For the thrill of the chase
For the opening act
For the mask to fall off soon after that

Please don't promise me
To gain favor
To gain trust
To have hope

Please stop
Because love can only
Tear me apart
Break promises

Burn bridges
Only so many times
Before I prefer the lone path
The darkness
Seeing the coldness of my breath
Feeling whatever is left
Before I'm left staring as people walk by
An empty vessel on the inside.

Chaotic Sanity

Don't chase after my heart
It's been broken and torn apart
Don't be that guy
Don't chase me
Don't want me
Don't need me
I just want you to be
You
Terrible
Imperfect
Wonderful
You
That's the guy I want to wake up next to
The light of my life
With an imperfect hue
I don't want to be chased
I don't want to be wanted
I don't want to be needed
I just want to be
Me
Terrible
Imperfect
Wonderful
Me
That's the woman I want you to see
The man and the woman we should
Always strive to be
The version of an imperfect reality

You and me
Imperfect
And
As perfect as can be.

Sex and Intimacy

Sex and intimacy
A twisted lyrical melody
Of words unspoken
Verbally
Of music discovered
Amusingly
Curling up listening to a song in my bed
A forever lasting melody in my head
Of a time
Of a place
Of a familiar face
The lyrics speak to my heart
The melody sings to my soul
Back to once upon a harmony
An everlasting dance
Tuned to
Sex and intimacy
Time has no measure
To the feelings of pleasure
The lyrical message
Whether a rite of passage
A distant memory
A loving symmetry
Put together
Piece by piece
From broken hearts

From broken dreams
Such is the consistency
Of sex and intimacy
A twisted lyrical melody.

Invisible Princess

He was once my dream
Too good to be true
Now he's your dream
An actual dream come true.

Legacy

Death wasn't
Significant
The people were

Death isn't
Significant
The people are.

Ocean View

You questioned your love for me
I questioned my love for you
That is how I knew
The earth had me
And the ocean had you.

After

I've been in love
With two natural disasters
One of these days
I'll build my home
And be safer
From anymore of those
But until then
I'm trapped in the
After
Aftermath
Aftertaste
Sea salt on my tongue
Smoke caught in my lungs
That's what's left
From the playful, moody ocean
From the passionate, irresistible fire
His amber eyed glow
Set me on fire
His storm gray eyes
Drowned me in his ocean
Two loves
Two natural disasters
Two eyes wiser after.

Blame Game

I want to punch a man
In the face
I see
My dad's face
My stepbrother's face
My first and second love's face
My dead love's face
As I'm tenderizing this poor man's face
Do I then pause
And realize
None of this was his fault in the first place.

Amor Fantasma

Dead and living
Numb and feeling
Grieving and healing
His death
Left a different kind of feeling
It's one thing to accept
The death of a relation
Of a friend
But this death
His death
Is a heartache that will never end
I miss his touch
I miss his smile
I miss how he loved me, if only for awhile
He had my heart
He had my love
He had me
All of me
More than I ever thought to believe
Dead and living
Numbing and feeling
Grieving and healing
His death
Left a different kind of feeling.

Anxiety

I'm tired of the words that I write
They feel like knives
Embedded in my heart
I crave a new start
I'm tired of
Loving
Caring
Giving
Feeling
Bleeding
I'm tired of my heart
Ripping
Tearing
Bruising
Crying
Breaking
Trying to mend it
Only for it to fall apart
I'm tired of the words that I write
They feel like knives
Embedded in my heart.

Damaged Treasure

I will not cave into you
You live in a shallow cave
It's treasure that you crave
Baubles and rubies
Sapphires
Whatever will take you higher
And you took my rare gold piece
Kept it
Took what you needed
Dulling my shine
Chewing up my worth
Spitting me out, content
Until I retreated
Rolled away towards the banks of the sand
Got swept up into the ocean
Sinking below to the deep end
Whoever finds my gold piece
Again
Will know by its shine
The light I managed to keep alive
That this gold piece has served its time.

Brittiny Gardner

From Me to You

I hope this poem
Reaches from me to you

For you to understand
That I still love you
Despite what you put me through
In the beginning
Towards the middle
At the end

The little girl inside of me
Now extends her arm
Holding out an olive branch
Asking for another chance
Hoping there's still time
To try again
The little girl inside of me
She forgives you
She wants to start anew

I hope this poem
Reaches from me to you

Because from me to you
It wasn't easy
Whenever I saw you
You never saw me
Instead, you saw a version of who you always wanted to be

Because of that, you chose
To use your love against me
Manipulate me
Like what you like
Do what you do
Where I thought you were loving me
You were honestly hurting me
Hurting the both of us
Causing the rift
Which even now is being mended
But our story doesn't have to end
Not like this
Not with the little girl inside crying raging fits

I hope this poem
Reaches from me to you

I still love you
I still hope for us
I still want to try
Because of you
I am me
I have learned to set my own self free
I hope you take this olive branch
And give us another chance

From me to you
I hope this poem reaches.

Messy Endings

It was just you and me
Us
Against all the zombies
Against all the ghosts of our pasts
Against all the odds

It was just you and me
Us
Making plans
Making memories
Making messes

It was just you and me
Us
Living for each other
Living in the moment
Living for the future to come

It was just you and me
Us
The journey was a messy one
The reality a terrible mess
The fantasy one a fun mess

It was just you and me
Us
Until it was just me
Until the world stopped
Until you walked away

Leaving me to clean the mess up.

Crash and Burn

It was a tragic crash
But it was the aftermath
That undid it all

A hopeful woman
Preparing her future
A hopeless fiancée
Staring at her ring
During the hard days.

And then August came around
She'll never forget that painful sound
The one that caused her
Mind to freeze
That brought her to her knees
That caused her heart to drop
Her whole world stopped

A sinking feeling
A sinking reality
3 fatalities
Two strangers
And a teenager she knew
One she befriended
One she had to carry
To the reefers
Below the mess decks

She still remembers
His voice
His laugh

She still remembers
The memorial
His best friend's letter

She'll never forget
The roll call
Where she dared to hold back
Her tears
They called muster
And his voice
They knew
They'd never hear

It was a tragic crash
But it was the aftermath
That undid it all

She lost her motivation
After that day
She lost her engagement
After that week
She had nightmares
She could barely sleep

Nearly three years later
He still haunts her dreams
This bright young teenager
Who coked n joked with her
And the other marines

26 were in the Osprey
23 survived
3 were frozen
For a time

Stories were swapped
The what ifs
The should've
Could've
Would've beens

3 years later
She shares her tragedy
She shares her aftermath
She shares her vulnerability
That she
Is me
And this happened
August 05, 2017
Forever imprinted in my memory.

Daydreaming

I dream of the grass
The sand
I dream of smelling flowers
Of smelling the earth again

I wake to watch
Day and night
I see the sea
It doesn't feel right

I miss the feel of the sand
Squished beneath my feet
I miss the earthy scent
The one that calls me back home to land

All I yearn for these days
Is the possibility
The hope
To touch land, to smell the flowers on the beach.

Blossom

I came upon a flower one day
It was colorful
It was pretty
I wanted it
I didn't know why
So I plucked it
And it died

I came upon another flower a month later
It was colorful
It was pretty
It was thorny
And I tried to pluck it
Its thorns bit me
I bled
I pulled harder
I continued to bleed down the stem
When I finally let go
I was left with a scar and a lesson.

I came upon another flower years later
It was pretty
It was colorful
I wanted to help it grow
So I watered it
I fed it
I nurtured it
Then when nothing happened days later
I watered it more

I fed it more
More and more
I went to the flower to help it grow
Only to see it had died
By overwatering and over feeding it
It suffocated from the inside.

By the time my heart had scarred
My soul had built its walls
My mind protected me from flowers
Altogether
I knew I was bitter
I knew I wasn't learning
I knew I was in misery
I knew I was a victim of my own doing

When age and wisdom finally caught up
When I realized I still wanted a flower
I knew it would be different this time
I had learned
Not to simply pluck
Not to grab onto biting thorns
Not to overwater/ overfeed
When I came upon my last flower
It was pretty
It was colorful
It was growing on its own
It wanted to be loved
It carried no thorns
So I admired it
And walked away.

Brittiny Gardner

Beautiful Wings

I am like a butterfly
I am ugly and unlearned
For a time
Eventually I build my own cocoon
I isolate and breathe
I ponder
I learn
Within my own mind
Within my own heart
Within my own soul
After a time
I blossom
I break out of my cocoon
And I spread my newfound wings
Newfound knowledge
Newfound strength
Newfound purpose
Bringing with me hope
I am like a butterfly
I do not see my beauty
I do not know my worth
But I do know
When I spread small joy
Unto people
I am happier
I do know
Wherever I go
I leave an impression

Overtime
I learn my worth
I see my own beauty within
And I know I am dying
My life is fleeting
So like a butterfly
That fears capture
You can see me
You can know me
You can learn from me
But you can never claim me
Unless I come back to you
That is how I know
I am like a butterfly.

What if...

Sometimes I'll stare at a mirror
My reality
My life
It all transparently clear
Who I am
Who I want to be
Such an easier concept in a parallel reality

Society is a metal detector
It's a mirror we are forced to see
People are transparent
Only when they choose to be
There are standards
There are expectations
There are stipulations
And they all fit in the back of a wagon

Like sheep herded into a crowd
Like wolves tricking the sheep
We wear our faces
We hide ourselves
We stay in the back
We watch the endless roads
And trees
And houses
And ever changing skies
Living our lies

What happens when one leaves the norm?
What happens when one decides enough is enough?
What happens when one person breaks their mirror?
Shatters it so much
That it's embedded into their skin
As a reminder
A piece of what they gave up
An end to eternal suffering

What if that one person chose to
Create
Innovate
Write
Draw
Paint
Sing
Play an instrument

What if they shared it with the world
Spreading love
Spreading joy
In a mirrored nightmare

Of standards
Of expectations
Of stipulations

What if the world could accept change
And shovel up the broken glass
And begin anew

What if...

The Call of the Beloved

I want to wrap my legs
Around your guitar body
Strum my fingers on the strings
Of your heart
Let my lyrics from my soul
Hold us together
Make us one and whole
My song
Your melody
A beautiful instrument of humanity.

Blink of a Tearful Eye

I don't know what hurts more
Loving you while you're here
But you don't remember me
Or loving you when you're gone
And I'm the one who hurts too much remembering you.

Tethered Art

Our thread
Tuned and timed
By the soul and the divine
Ever your Blossom
Ever my Loki
Ink and paint
Our key
To unlocking our story.

Once Upon A Log Cabin

It all started while dreaming up a log cabin
Where things did and didn't happen
Where I ate a lotus flower
And became more empowered
In this potential safe haven
Times of bliss
Kisses and lust permits
Secret nights to remember
To trust and surrender
And to think it all happened
Once upon a log cabin.

Broken Record

A father's love
A mother's love
That's all a child ever really thinks about
That's all I've wanted since I was young
But the cards said no
The tears said no
One way or the other
I watched them both go
Their separate ways
What can I say
My father just left
My mother shut down
Left me bereft
My siblings and I tried
Living our own lives
But still the craving persisted
Even as I resisted
Time went by
Life continued on
And still I replay
This broken record
Of a song.

Hopeful Tomorrow

Hope still thrives
Through the deepest of sorrows
May we have a better tomorrow
Enjoy the present
For it's a gift
The future untold
Of tangled truths and myths.

Best Friend

Be your own happiness
Be your own love
Be your own trust
Be your own safety.

....

How can I let you in?

When I can't even let myself in?

....

Life's Full of Lies

Life's full of lies
It's up to us to accept or deny
The truth over the lie
Death holds the secrets and the truth
Life leads the blind; present the roots
We blossom and die
Ashes to ashes
Dust to dust
We'll rise and burn like fire
Watch as the flames soar higher
Ground ourselves and plant the seed
Life's full of lies
Hope is what thrives
What we crave is what we bleed
A loud yet silent scream
Truth and lies
Life and death
Each of these ends with a final breath.

. . . .

When you exist to simply EXIST
then you have given up on living.
To live is to learn, to love, to have meaning
and purpose. If you exist to just be —
then you're already dead.

. . . .

Sealed Shut

I loved you too much
More than enough
And when you didn't need me anymore
You chose to walk out that door
Causing me to still
Painfully love you harder than I ever did before.

All of Me

I gave you everything
Said I would do anything
But in the end
I really owed you nothing.

Bleeding Heart

My heart continues to bleed
And through the bleeding
It is felt
And it is seen
All I'm asking is to love and be loved in
Return
But at the same time, I'd rather feel the pain and the
Burns

Prince Who?

I don't wanna be your secret lover
I don't wanna be your forbidden fantasy
I don't wanna be your kiss don't tell
I don't wanna fall under your spell
I'm not a princess waiting to be
Swept off her feet
I'm the kind of girl you don't wanna meet
I carry a lot of baggage
I'm pretty heavily damaged
I don't believe in Happy Endings
I don't believe in destiny
So just hand me back my shoe
And I'll happily forget I ever met you
The End

....

I may never be good enough for you,
But I will be good enough for myself.

....

Love Before

Unconditional they say
Will forever stay
If that was the case
Why has mine frayed
Snapped off
Hit me
Added insult to injury
Only to go its own way

True love they say
Ha!
That belongs in
Books, movies, TV
True love is a fantasy
Meant to give false hope
And break young girl's hearts
Like me

Love conquers all they say
Love is a fallacy I say
It's branched all over
It's wicked and cruel
It plays games
Its full of mischief
Plays by its own rules
In the end, we all lose

Brittiny Gardner

Love During

Unconditional I have
Not forever but not temporary either
Now in my case
It's there when it can be
It's not always blood ties
Fostered through experience
Wisdom over lies
A second chance overtime

True love, I have
Just like the written pages
Sapped with tears and fears
An adventure unlike any other
True love is something
A song can never run out of tune
It's a once upon a time
Happily ever after good bye

Love, I have
As I age, I understand
This four letter word
Has so much power
Has so much value
Has so much to learn from
Love isn't always an enemy.

Love After

Unconditional they say
Will forever stay
I say
True
It's there in sight
It's deep in roots
It's held in the night sky
It's painted in the morning sunrise

True love they say
No more haughty laughter
True love is what I am after
I've had my share of the platter
I've seen the blossoming of intimacy
I've held onto someone I've loved
I've learned to simply believe

Love conquers all they say
Love used to be a fallacy to me
Now I understand
Now I've had so much of it
Now I crave nothing but it
Love leads me to believe
In a dangerous adventure worth risking.

Self

I'm holding hands with
My past self
My present self
My future self

I'm looking at
My past self
My present self
My future self

I'm understanding
My past self
My present self
My future self

All else, I'm loving
My past self
My present self
My future self.

Torn Sweater

For some
Love is meant to be worn
Not kept
For others
Like myself
Love is meant to be kept
Not worn.

Adulting

Younger
I needed you more
And missed you less
Older
I need you less
And miss you much more.

Memoir

My past is the spine
My present the cover
My future the chapters I've yet to write
But where it feels real
Where it feels heard
It's all simple poetry
It's all a novel fantasy
My life is a book
Of who
Of where
Of what
I want to be
And all it's missing
Is who
Is where
Is what
Person I want to spend the rest of my pages with.

Musing

I really am a muse
A powerful inspiration
But never lasting
In the artist's heart.

Camouflage

I don't want you to know
I wear steel toed boots
And dog tags to show
Where my body is supposed to go
I want you to know me
To look me in the eyes
And see my beautiful poetry
To hold my hands
And run with me
As we explore all the foreign lands
Of a modern fantasy
To hold me tight
Through the darkest of storms
To keep my heart
Secure and warm
I don't want you to see
The perception of what makes me
Me
I just want you to feel
That what I am
That what makes me
Me
The perspective is what's real
So when you try on my shoes
Know that they're not just steel toed boots.

Sparks

When you know
You know
Until then
People will continue
To come and go.

An Ugly Kind of Pretty

Pretty people
Believe ugly is real
Ugly people
Believe pretty is imaginary
When a pretty person
Looks in a mirror
She feels flaws
She feels claws
She feels the withdrawal
She feels
What society
Calls
Ugly
When an ugly person
Looks in a mirror
She sees flaws
She sees claws
She sees the withdrawal
She doesn't see
What society
Calls
Pretty

Siren Song

I'll be your siren
Sitting on the rock
Staring at your ship at sea
When you're on the watch
Listen for me
I'll sing you our song
Of eternal love
Watch as it washes you
Back into the deep
Back to your eternal sleep.

Ageless Eyes

The eyes see all
They don't change their size
Perhaps their color
But never size
They stay
Young
Old
Wise
They're the windows
To the soul
They're what keeps
Us hopeful and whole.

Te Extrano

Are you a ghost
Are you a soul
Are you in limbo
Where did you go
Some days
I hear you
I feel you
I see you
Everyday
I miss you
I cry over you
I die a little more inside
Why
Why is it the young
To leave
To be deceived
To have fate
To have destiny
Mock and cut
Their fated line
It's not fair
I'll never understand why
Why the young must die.

Mi Corazon y Estrella

I'm North
You're South

I'm winter's promise
You're summer's bliss

I'm white as bread
You're a tatted Mexican

I had immeasurable fall
You had Texas skies you'd share on your phone
I'm tall
You're short

I read for fun
You studied teeth for the long run

See
We're as different as can be

But this Yankee
Fell in love with a Texan

A deep rooted Mexican
Preaching Texan

With a heart of gold
And a soul as blossoming as the Yellow Tea Rose

I was a dork
So were you

I escaped in books
So did you

I played videogames
So did you

I spoke deep thoughts
So did you

In a world away from home
Away from what we know

We found each other
Through the laughter

Through the tears
Through the love

Over the years
Highs and lows

Songs and memories
Though you're gone from here

You're still with me
Now and always

One dork to another
We've always been true

One deep soul to another
We'll see each other again

One love to another
Heaven is another distance

One gamer to another
I let you win

One reader to another
The best part of any book is the open ending

I'm glad to have
Met you
Loved you
Held you

I'm glad you
Met me
Loved me
Held me

As different as we were
We were more similar than I can
Ever express through words

Just know
You touched my heart
Mi Corazon
Mi Estrella
And I've never been the same.

Tempting Aquarius

Two hearts pulled asunder
Ocean eyes
Murky waters
Shades of blue
Shades of gray
Collaborate
Into the storm of the century
That's how I feel
When you look at me
Our lips meet
Against the crashing of the waves
We're pulled apart
Led astray
Back on land
Your current pulls me
Back to you again
Lost at sea
Drowning in your memory.

Dead Doll's Heart

It's just those feelings
It's just that craving
It's just that connection
Having it and losing it
Needing it and not finding it
A painful reminder
The worst pain I'll ever name
A broken heart
A mending heart
Tearing me apart
Like death just lost its game
That heartache is worse than leaving this world
Through this pain I'll never come back the same
Who I used to be
Naïve
Who I wanted to be
An adult
Who I can never be
A social butterfly
Who he showed me I could be
A free spirit
It's his heartbeat
It's his hair
It's his love
That I desperately crave
That I'll now take to the grave
The withdrawals
The memories

The painful mind numbing reality
The untold secrets we both never shared
I have to now pretend like I never cared
Let death deal its medicine
My heart will help it along
I'm a dead doll now
In a world I'll never understand
It's just those feelings
It's just that craving
It's just that connection
A broken heart
A mending heart
Tearing me apart
Its his heartbeat
It's his hair
It's his love
The withdrawals
The memories
The painful mind-numbing reality.

Spider and the Fly

I know what you are
But I don't know who you are
Which leaves me
In constrained ignorance

You're magnetic
They all are

You're creative
They all are

You're insatiable
They all are

You're passionate
They all are

So why
I know what you are
I know your kind
So why
Why do I still try

It's like I enjoy being burned
Being used
Being hurt

It's like I can't get enough
Of the drug
Of the high

It's like I can't resist
The depth of us both

The blanket of honesty
It's like you're the spider
And I'm the gullible fly

It's like I'm the curious moth
And you're the enticing flame

It's like we're both players
In a never ending game

I know what you are
You're magnetic
You're creative
You're insatiable
You're passionate

But I don't know who you are
And that's the major difference
That is what urges me to try
You're a different kind of high

You're a new player
In a familiar game
I wonder

If I am the fly
If I am the moth
Will it end the same way

Or will I
Find the will
Find the courage
Find the sense
To turn around
And fly away…

Sorry Not Sorry

I'm sorry
I have to
Hate myself
In order to fix myself
I have to
Love myself
In order
To accept myself
That I need both
To feel complete
To feel free
To know my imperfections
Are what make up me
And you know what
I'm not sorry

Afterthoughts

I always wondered
Whether you were better off
With me no longer
Your motivation
Your support
Your love
For me
Without your motivation
Without your support
Without your love
It's been painful
I haven't felt better off
It's been loss
And then discovery
This never ending recovery
I still
Love you
Hate you
Confuse you
I go back and forth
Beginning to understand my worth
That though we're long done
Forgiveness helps us carry on
Through the years
There's been
 much pain
much tears
smiles masking the fear
I always wondered

Whether you were better off
With me no longer
Your motivation
Your support
Your love
But now I want you to be happy
Because we are our
Own motivation
Own support
Own love
I don't wonder anymore
This was never our forever
But we can find
Our own chance at happiness again.

Cherished Madness

Though it was temporary
It was extraordinary
From the depths of my soul
I blissfully fell down the rabbit hole
I saw colors
I smelled ambrosia
I tasted passion
I heard songs
I felt alive
And when he left
When I woke from my reverie
When the hopes were tragedies
When the love wasn't enough anymore
I found my way back to reality's door
Like Alice once curious then learned
I walked out of there
Blissfully ignorant and burned.

The Scorpion's Sting and the Virgin's Rising

When the scorpion
Stings a virgin's heart
She convulses
She bleeds
Her heart ashen
Her eyes sparked
Her mind made up
She breathes
She cries with joy
She bleeds slower
When the virgin's heart
Rises anew
That Scorpion will understand
He lost not only her love
But also gained her wrath
To kill with kindness
Her chosen path
Karma will deliver
The virgin's innocence bled
Once the scorpion wanted her dead
Now she's risen
He's in a fragile position
Will she be merciful
Or will she deliver him
To death's door
Or break his heart forever more
Like he broke hers
When he stung her cold
When he knifed her hot

When he left her body to rot
Death was too good for him
So she decided to sting him
In the mind
Led him and his generations
To be manically inclined
Left her virgin heart at his dying side
Poetic
Tragic
Ironic
Because we're all a little mad sometimes.

....

The Unbreakable Girl
Who Never Stopped

....

Brittiny Gardner

Alive in Your Eyes

I miss your eyes
Dark like the night sky
Holding all the stars
That's where you are

And I miss his blue eyes
Deeper than the sea
The way that they'd
Always laugh with me

And I miss his brown eyes
That amber eyed glow
Showing the fire's burning higher
Much higher than we both know

And I miss her hazel eyes
They were once innocent and childlike
But they've lived through a longer time
They've aged and intensified

They've loved
They've lost
All at a great cost

I miss all of these passionate eyes
The core of their love I carry on the inside
The stars, the seas, the fires
The tears I still cry on the outside

Kindred

Angel wings
Angel skies
Angel eyes
It's not
Hi, nice to meet you
It's
Where have you been!
Connection
Recognition
Reincarnation
The soul
The heart
The mind
Like a mirror
You and I
Welcome home
I'll help you inside.

All or Nothing

All I want to hear is
I want you
I choose you
I love you
This I can guarantee
But all I hear is
I don't know
I've been hurt a lot
It's not you, it's me
I can't give you a guarantee
What about now
How do you feel
About us now
About us together
Today
Tomorrow
The near future
It's a maybe venture
It's a passing tide
It's a tiresome rollercoaster of a ride
All I want to hear is
I want you
I choose you
I love you
This I can guarantee
Unfortunately, this isn't my reality.

Sober Love

Sober love
Sober memories
Sober kisses
Sober laughter
Sober time
Sober feelings
Sober hours
Sober love
What the hell made me give it all up?
Why the hell did I give you up?
Who I was when I was with you I loved being
When we hung out time was fleeting
Wherever we go from this
I already know
We will both sorely miss this
Sober love
More painful
More vital
More real
Than that temporary heal
Than that ecstasy of a drug
Than that passing great love
Sober love
Why did I give you up?

Sweet Nothings

The ecstasy
Of your beautiful lies
The way you drew me in
The way you spun my mind
The way you felt all over
The intensity
Of this dangerous high
Always ends
Always leaves me crying
Always wakes me up
The ecstasy
The intensity
The ugliness in your eyes
I dismiss
As your voice drips
Beautiful lies

Doll Eyed Enchantment

She feels like a circus act
As your eyes watch her
Dance up on the pole
Watch her eyes roll back
When you feel that clap back
From her icy eyed stare later on
When she makes love
It's raw and passionate
Like she's searching
Like she's wanting
Like she's giving you her soul
But when she's fucking
It's physical
It's primal
It's a fight over all
In her head
In her heart
All the tears
Turned to rage
So when you witness her circus act
When she's put on display
As her doll like eyes
Pierce your ignorant ones
Understand that she's just lost in her head
She doesn't see you
She sees right through you
She isn't with you
The circus act
The pole dance

Making love
Fucking high
Her eyes roll back towards the sky
Forever searching
Forever wanting
Forever giving her soul
But you'll never know her past the pole.

Dreamscape

She called it
A getaway
He called it
Peace
Both agreed
It was a natural release
Underground history
Uplifting scenery
Unique personalities
Shared with a weekend of bliss
Sweet kisses
Sweet laughter
Sweet nostalgia soon after
It all felt too surreal
Like a dream
She called it
A getaway
He called it
Peace
Both agreed
It was a natural release.

All Bottled Up, All Broken Down

My heart aches
My moods swing
My mind's cracking
and my soul is tearing
someone took the bottles
someone broke the shelf
that helped me maintain my functioning self
Now I'm spiraling
Now I'm hurting
Now I'm drowning
All over again
My life
My past
My present
Back on the damn insane wagon
All over again
My heart aches
For them
For time
For peace
My moods swing
From time to time
From the past saying hi
From the present trying to ground itself
My mind's cracking
Morals are shifting
Morals I knew: ethics and pathos
Morals over acceptance today
My soul is tearing

Has been since I was a child
Has been since I witnessed death
Has been since life has left me more bereft
Sometime
Someone
Something
Stole my bottles
Broke my shelf
That once helped me maintain my functioning self.

Icicle

This page is as blank as my mind.
Words slowly form onto the ruled lines.
Images filter from my mind to the page.
A dancing snowflake
A crying daughter bent on her knees
A knife slowly raised, then lowered.
Plunging deep into a frozen heart
Screaming in agony
The knife twisting
The pain worsening
Her mother finished at last
Sheathing her tongue
Her constant companion
Her only weapon
Listening to her daughter cry.
The daughter felt her heart harden
Felt her blood boil
Knew her pain was her only weapon
And she wouldn't let it bother her, not anymore.
Just her, alone, she prayed
Wishing her life to be better someday.
She fell asleep
Tears streaming down her face
Dreaming of a safer place
And the snow continued to fall
Without a care at all
The cold was her new friend

The ice
The storm inside of her
A blizzard that helped freeze her hurting heart
An icicle her new numbing counterpart.

Sea Hearts

The pressure contracts
But you hold your composure
You and your crew, shoulder to shoulder
Blaring alarms, and sharp, shrill piping
Everyone listening
They spring into action
They pledge their lives to the sea
They fight for their ship
They sweat and they bleed
Cacophony of yells and commands
Hand over hand
Ship and man
Together, both can
Together, both will.

Isolate

I'm tired
I'm hurt
I feel naked
My heart's been raped again
My soul left unhinged
My body craving sanctuary
Wanting to be alone again
I'm tired
I'm hurt
I feel lost
My heart's been used again
My soul lied to
My body left in pain
Wishing it would all go away.

I Have A Dream

As a child
I was told to keep dreaming
That one day it would become
My reality
As an adult now
I'm told to stop dreaming
That this is
My reality.

Always Temporary

She enjoyed it
While it lasted
He left, eventually
As was expected
They always leave
They never stay
Deep down inside
She secretly feared
It would always
Be this way.

Imperfection is Perfection

Sometimes you must
Break a little
Cry a little
Die a little
Fall apart a little
In order to heal
Because this, this is real.
Who you are, is important.
Who you want to be, is your pathway.
Who everyone sees are your landmarks
Who you are inside is all that matters
To love yourself
To understand yourself
To believe in yourself
Is the journey's center to the earth
And earth is nature
And nature is human
And human is erred
To err is human
And humanity is flawed
A perfect flow
In an imperfect world.

Fed Up

All your pretty lies
I don't believe them anymore
So go on
Walk out that door
All your pretty lies
Have left me dead inside
Unless you give me
Some proof
Some bit of the truth
Shhhh
I don't want to hear another word
Until you show me the effort
I know I deserve
So take your pretty lies
And get the fuck out of my life.

I Found the Answer

Pretty lies
Plus
Pretty cries
Minus
Pretty smiles
Plus
Hidden tears
Multipy
Forgotten fears
Plus
Hardened hearts
Equals
A fresh start
Finally solved the
Equation of a broken heart.

Karma's Kiss

A broken person
Doesn't want to
Be heard
Be held
Be healed
They want to wear Hell Fire
Touch every soul who broke them
With karma's kiss
A sickening twist of forgiveness
A broken person
Doesn't want to
Be missed
No
Oh no
They want their own form of justice.

Grief is Eternal

Go ahead
Beat me up physically
Slice my soul with your words
Let me grab my bandages
Both internal and external
At least you'll still be there tomorrow
At least we'll be able to say sorry and make up
At least we'll have time to heal
But please…please don't ever leave me
Don't die
So I'm left to grieve your absence
Grief is the worst pain there ever is
You can't reconcile it
You can't bandage it
You can only go through the process
The true core of sufferance.

Aloha

I hear The Past
The crying
The laughter
The yelling
The Nostalgia calling me
"Stay and remember,"
But I put up one hand
"I can visit, but I can never stay,"
Nostalgia frowns
The Past sighs
But they both understand why
If I stayed with The Past
I'd never let go and move forward
I'd be stuck in and left in Nostalgia's smothering embrace.
Calling it another phase
Until the agony pulls me in further
To stay
And never learn to forgive and walk away.

To Be Continued...

You were like
A new release
Displayed on the shelf
I needed to have you
All to myself
I saw your title
I wasn't afraid
I read your book jacket
Was left more amazed
I wanted to read every line
To understand your story
So you could maybe one day relate to mine
But like all good books
Yours came to an end
Left on a cliffhanger
And I knew right then
That I was your chapter
That I'd be your muse
I'd help you continue
The sequel to you
A whole new part
A whole new setting
A whole new life
Something that was ours
Something we'd both understand
Something we'd both look back on time and again
Unfortunately
Our story never finished
It simply ended

I never got to see past the cliffhanger
Of you
You never got to see past the cliffhanger of me
We just weren't meant to combine
Our stories
We just weren't meant to bind our pages together
We just weren't meant for happily ever after.

If the love hurts like hell,
then you show them what they lost.

From Me

. . .

You'll never know
If you don't ask.
You'll never learn
If you don't try.

. . .

Manifest good in your life – stop running back to what you know; that isn't comfort, that isn't love. That is routine.
That is insanity.

Her Fantasy

He wanted to suck out her soul
He wanted her to moan loudly
He wanted her to tease him, to please him
He wanted her body
He desired her

She wanted to suck him dry
She wanted him to moan loudly
She wanted to taste his flavor, for him to touch her all over
She wanted his body
She craved him

Both entwined
Both caught up in a water dance
Of sweat and release
Of passion and fun
And when she woke up
Tears stained on her pillow
She painfully wondered if it really happened
Or if it was all a fantasy in her head
A love story that had no beginning or an end.

Leave

Don't stay
Go away
I don't need another lesson
I don't need another "Maybe Boat,"
Take your words
Take your boat
Take your own manipulated heart
And go the fuck away
I'm tired—and I no longer want for you to stay.

Thank You

I want to thank
Those who left me
Those who lied to me
Those who mind fucked me
Because of all of you
I know that
It's ok
To walk away
It's ok
To play both sides
It's ok
To stay OR leave
It's ok
To choose ME.

PAST

I wish that I could tell my younger self
That it's going to be ok
That Christmas time won't come every day
That each year
While we're in the dark and swimming in tears
There's still some light
Some hope that's shining our way

I wish that I could tell my younger self
That momma doesn't mean the words
She yells
That her pain is just as bitter as our own
Our histories have tethered in a painful form

I wish that I could tell my younger self
That daddy didn't mean to set the fire
All our childhood memories meant more to him than he desired
Back then
And now he's watching the ashes dance in the wind

I wish that I could tell my younger self
That reading was the way to be our true self
That it is ok to let people into our fucked-up world as well
That it is ok to have our voice heard; we have quite the story to tell.

I wish that I could tell my younger self
That loving yourself is where it's at
That the pain of the past

It – it doesn't have to last
That even though right now it feels like we're going nowhere fast
We should take the time to make lasting memories
For we are our own dead and living history.

PRESENT

I need to tell my present self
To get a grip and run like the wind
To leave the doubters and the haters
In the dust
To run wild and free
Simply embrace yourself
Decide who you want to be

I need to tell my present self
That it's ok to make mistakes
That life is all for it
Thrives off it
Learns because of it
Progresses and declines
Balances over time
Mistakes are progressive.

I need to tell my present self
To stop self-hating
To stop self doubting
To stop the inner dance within yourself
To say your pleasantries and be done
To risk it all because you'll finally see
You have won.

FUTURE

I wish that I could tell my future self
That my present life is dancing with its past
That the present doesn't root me
But it leaves me in a lotus reverie
That when I wake will leave me in misery

I wish that I could ask my future self
Does it all finally add up
Does the pain finally go away
Does the love exist that I crave
Does happiness exist in my life to that very day?

I wish that I could ask my future self
Did I finally untether myself
Did I finally break the cycle
Did I finally change my own stars
Did I finally choose for myself?

....

Life is a teacher. It's meant to teach you, inspire you, help you one day out master the teacher by sharing your wisdom with the future so that they can continue paying it forward. And it is from there, that getting old is a gift.

....

Fuckboys Tell All Tales

Pretty eyes
Pretty Smile
Their lies could extend for miles
Pretty hair
Pretty face
It's their memory I trace and retrace
Those heated moments
The pleasure and the pain
A temporary salve
You'd think I'd learn
You'd think I'd evolve
You'd think I'd leave before they did
Inevitably
That
I'd finally stop crying
I'd finally stop caring
I'd finally stop craving
The pleasurable pain
Something about a Fuckboy
Fucking with my brain
Fucking with my mind
Fucking with my insides
The way my eyes
Watch their lips pucker
Watch their body move with mine
Watch their expressions
Feel their lips on mine
Feel them inside me
Feel their skin slick with sweat

Hear their moans
Hear their dirty promises
Hear their sweet nothings
That turn into a string of lies
Pretty eyes
Pretty smiles
Pretty hair
Pretty face
Out of body adventures
Heartburn thereafter
Ugh
What makes these bad boys so special
Why am I such a sucker for a Fuckboy special…

Tick Tock, You Really Thought...

You chose your life
Now I'm choosing mine
We were like hands on a clock
We'd meet up
Last a whole minute
That felt like a lifetime
That was gone too fast
That was gone too soon
Tick tock
You'd have my heart race
You'd have my head rock
You'd have my soul begging
All I ever wanted was safety
But you were the opposite
You were a toxic high
A breath of fresh air
In a world that doesn't care
And for a short while
I felt wanted
I felt desired
I felt loved
Tick tock
The hands separate
Over before it starts
Such is the matters
Of a damaged heart
Of a broken mind
Of a bitter soul
You chose your life

Now I'm choosing mine
Tick tock
We'll meet up again
We always do
A humorous fate
The longest minute of our lives
Or the shortest seconds of time
Tick tock
Like the hands on a clock.

Fated Use

It's fun to be a muse
In the beginning
To know you're the
Inspiration
 Magic touch
The thirst the artist slakes
But later
Through the art
You see a truth you can't deny
The simple spelling
The one word involved
M-U-S-E
A man's inspiration
A man's entertainment
A man's temporary flame
Until the one word
Spoils the rest of the game
When a muse is
No longer a muse
She's been burned
She's just tired
She's been used
Use
Now how amused are we?
You pity the fool
I pity the muse in me.

Estrellas y Mariposas

All I need
Are the butterflies during the day
Are the stars shining in the night sky
To know that
You and I
Are okay

All I want
Is your heart next to mine
Your breath in my ear
And waking up to your smile year after year

Just you and I
And
Stars and butterflies
All I want.

Trained

One is reason
One is passion
And all you want
Is to take action
But instead
You take flight
Because it's what
You know to be right.

Imposter Syndrome

I don't feel like myself
Am I
Myself?
This skin doesn't feel like mine
My breath doesn't feel like mine
My mind feels tangled
This heart in my chest
It ticks
It beats
It pulses
I'm full of impulses
Is this me now?
This voice
Feels lost
Feels new
This body
Is it mine?
How old am i
What year is it
Why is it that at certain times
I feel like a changeling
Exchanged for someone
More pure
More normal
More gifted
The only thing that ever feels
That ever truly belongs
To me
And only me

No matter
The body
The heart
The mind
The voice
Are my eyes
My aged
Yet ageless
Empathetic
Hazel eyes
They're the only thing
That I can claim are mine
While the rest of me are borrowed body parts
Just waiting for their replacement date
Everyone's a whore
We just sell different parts of ourselves
And so, it will be forevermore
In this nevermore
Evermore…

Don't Put A Ring On It

Some of us prefer the chase
Not all of us wanna end up
With a ring in our face
We've had our heart shattered
 all over the place
our mind and soul scattered
out all over outer space
some of us prefer the
sprint part of the race
we enjoy the pleasure and the pain
before disappearing without a trace.

Pleading Angel

I'm dying while being alive
I've never had anything feel like it was mine
Always felt stuck on a shelf
Used like a toy
To bring temporary feelings of pain and joy
Then tossed
Then lost
Then broken all over again
But do I ever *truly* break?
Not in person
I fight to this day
But at night
When I'm lost
In my thoughts
In my dreams
I see her over and over
The broken soul version of me
Her wings torn
Her eyes bleeding black ink
Her skin pure ivory
And all she does
Is cry
Is howl in agony
And when I'm awake
With the fake smile over my face
In the mirror
I see her again

through my eyes
As the eyes are the windows to the soul
And as the tears flow
I wonder if I'll ever again feel whole.

Existing

I speak
No one listens
I cry
No one hears
I lie
No one bats an eye.

I'm that invisible
I'm that innocent
I'm that "Here"

I scream
In my head
I love
In my heart
I bleed
In my soul
I fake smile
In the mirror

I'm here
But not here

This Is for You

I've given enough
I've had enough
I will never be good enough
For you
But I will be enough for myself
And that's the sweetest vengeance
I could ever put you through.

The Victor Not The Victim

Take your narcissistic tears
Cry them to a different pair of ears

Take your bipolar mind
And offload it to another of your kind

One personality, two
All twenty can stay over there with you

You took advantage
Of me
You expected too much
Of me
Thought I was just gonna lie down and
Take it
Well I've finally had enough

So take it all
Here's your emotional bag
Your trauma
Your drama
Your dad and your mama
Just get it out of my face
Because where you continue
To cry
To lie
To hide
To blame everyone
Except who you are on the inside

I'll be living my best life
I'll be free of
Your narcissism
Your personality disorders
Your bipolar disorder
I'll be making moves
Building my life away from yours
Burning the bridge I fought so hard
To keep afloat
To salvage
To form and reform
I'm done compromising
I'm finally realizing
I won't be you
I won't drown myself in the past
I won't victimize myself anymore
No
I will be me
I will be the victor, the cycle breaker
Of this generational curse
For better or for worse.

From Me to You: Fuck You

I don't wanna be
a princess anymore
I finally shut that damn door
I wanna wear that villainous cape
Wear dark eyeliner
Sharpen my glittering eyes
Full of malice
As I sip from my evil chalice
I wanna watch everybody
From
My past
My present
My nearby future
Beg for mercy
Beg and plead on their knees
Begging while saying pretty please
To which I'll laugh in their face
Remind them of a certain time and place
Watch the recognition glean over their fake innocent faces
And I'll smile evilly
And reply
Ever so sweetly
Darling, if you'd just listened to me back then, we wouldn't be here in the first place.
But alas
As I tip back my glass

I knew this was coming
Once I let **her** out of her cage
The Selfish Villainous Age
And she's here to STAY.

Contents

colophon
Brought to you by Wider Perspectives Publishing, care of James Wilson, with the mission of advancing the poetry and creative community of Hampton Roads, Virginia.
This page used to have many cute and poetic expressions, but the sheer number of quality artists deserving mention has superseded the need to art. This has become some serious business; please check out how *They art...*

Tabetha Moon House
Travis Hailes- Virgo, thePoet
Nick Marickovich
Grey Hues
Rivers Raye
Madeline Garcia
Chichi Iwuorie
Symay Rhodes
Tanya Cunningham-Jones
(Scientific Eve)
Terra Leigh
Raymond M. Simmons
Samantha Borders-Shoemaker
Taz Weysweete'
Jade Leonard
Darean Polk
Bobby K.
(The Poor Man's Poet)
J. Scott Wilson (Teech!)
Charles Wilson
Gloria Darlene Mann
Neil Spirtas
Jorge Mendez & JT Williams
Sarah Eileen Williams
Stephanie Diana (Noftz)
Shanya – Lady S.
Jason Brown (Drk Mtr)
Ken Sutton

Kailyn Rae Sasso
Crickyt J. Expression
Se'Mon-Michelle Rosser
Lisa M. Kendrick
Cassandra IsFree
Nich (Nicholis Williams)
Samantha Geovjian Clarke
Natalie Morison-Uzzle
Gus Woodward II
Patsy Bickerstaff
Edith Blake
Jack Cassada
Dezz
M. Antoinette Adams
Catherine TL Hodges
Kent Knowlton
Linda Spence-Howard
Tony Broadway
Zach Crowe
Mark Willoughby
Martina Champion
... and others to come soon.

the Hampton Roads
Artistic Collective
(757 Perspectives) &
The Poet's Domain
are all WPP literary journals in cooperation with Scientific Eve or Live Wire Press

Check for those artists on FaceBook, Instagram, the Virginia Poetry Online channel on YouTube, and other social media.
Hampton Roads Artistic Collective is an extension of WPP which strives to simultaneously support worthy causes in Hampton Roads and the local creative artists.

Made in the USA
Middletown, DE
27 October 2023

41383278R00106